MW00642241

Best Christmas Ever

28 Practical Ways to Make This the Best Christmas of Your Life!

Matthew Kelly

PUBLISHED BY BLUE SPARROW
AN IMPRINT OF VIIDENT

To learn more about the author, visit:
MatthewKelly.com

ISBN: 978-1-63582-531-2 (softcover)

Designed by Todd Detering

10 9 8 7 6 5 4 3 2 1

FIRST EDITION

Printed in the United States of America

Table of Contents

1. Fail on Purpose. 1
2. Begin with Purpose. 5
3. Life is Short! 8
4. The Main Thing. 10
5. Temper Your Expectations. 12
6. Create Memories. 14
7. The Power of Anticipation. 17
8. Rediscover Childhood. 19
9. Learn to Do Nothing. 21
10. The Santa Question. 25
11. Be a Pilgrim, Not a Tourist! 28
12. Getting to Know Yourself. 34
13. That Difficult Conversation. 37
14. Escape the Joyless Urgency. 39
15. Listen to Music. 41
16. Stop Trying to Hack Life. 43
17. Learn to Deep Think. 45
18. Pay Attention. 48
19. Be Present Not Preoccupied. 51
20. Locate Your Heart. 53

21. Amazing Sundays. 57

22. Attend to Your Spiritual Illness. 59

23. Technology Fasting. 62

24. The Importance of Christmas PJs. 65

25. The Sights, Smells, and Sounds of Christmas. 67

26. Movie Night. 69

27. Acceptance and Surrender. 76

28. Everyone Knows that Love is the Only Way. 79

29. Holy Moments. 82

1.
Fail on Purpose.

"A place where everyone is striving for what isn't worth having." This is how Thackeray describes Vanity Fair in his novel of 1848. It aptly defines so much of our culture. "A place where everyone is striving for what isn't worth having." It also aptly describes the way many people approach Christmas each year. "A place where everyone is striving for what isn't worth having."

In the process we will cease striving for everything that isn't worth having and focus our efforts on the very few things that matter most, the things we should strive for with our whole hearts, minds, bodies, and souls.

#1. Decide to fail on purpose. I know it sounds crazy. It is completely counter intuitive. It is the opposite of what our success-focused, over-productive, achievement obsessed culture tells us ten million times throughout our lives.

What am I talking about? You cannot do everything. You cannot succeed at everything. You cannot be the best at everything. And despite what the culture would like you to believe, you cannot have it all.

You have to choose. You cannot play golf and tennis on Saturday afternoon. It's okay to fail. It's okay to miss out. We miss out on almost everything if you really stop to think about it. Every time you decide to do one thing, you are deciding not to do everything else. When you choose a career you choose not to pursue every other profession. When a man chooses to marry his wife, he doesn't think, "Oh, I am missing out on the other four billion women on the planet."

Our lives are forged with tough choices or wasted in indecision.

It's time to start intentionally neglecting things that don't matter. It's okay to fail at things that aren't important. It's necessary. It's wise. It's the only sane thing to do in a world full of unlimited options.

You fail every day. You are going to fail every day for the rest of your life. The key is to fail at the right things, to fail at the things that don't matter.

So, as you begin this journey toward Christmas, take a few minutes and identify what really matters.

Don't make a long list. This will just set you up to fail at what matters most and lead you to feel anxious, overwhelmed, and defeated.

Choose three things. What really matters this Christmas? Your three things might be:

1. Host a wonderful family gathering.

2. Have a powerful encounter with God on Christmas Day at Church.

3. Make this an amazing Christmas for someone else.

This kind of clarity is liberating. By getting clear about the most important things, you begin to realize that there are a great many things that it is okay to fail at because they don't matter that much. You can then decide what to intentionally neglect. You can decide what to intentionally fail at.

Whatever three you decide upon, keep them at the top of your to-do list as you journey toward Christmas this Advent.

You probably won't get it right the first time, and you can change it as you reflect more in the coming days, but resist the temptation to add to this list. Keep the list at three. There will be other important things, but these are the three most important things. If you want to put something else on the list, you need to take something off the list.

This simple three item list will help you remain clear about what matters most this Christmas.

Keep another list with the dozens of things you need to do to prepare for Christmas, but at every point between now and Christmas, be clear about the three things that matter most.

Every time you feel obliged, compelled, or guilted into doing something for Christmas, reflect on your top three priorities and ask yourself, "Am I giving these enough time and attention?"

"Things that matter most should never be at the mercy of things that matter least," was Goethe's observation, but we let it happen all the time. Decide, here and now, that this Christmas you will not let things that matter least rule over things that matter most.

If you want to have your Best Christmas Ever, begin by deciding what matters most, and then honor, celebrate, prioritize, and bask in those few things.

Release yourself from the tyranny of the trivial many and adopt the wisdom of the vital few.

2. Begin with Purpose.

Welcome back to Best Christmas Ever! We are going to explore twenty-eight ways to make this your Best Christmas Ever!

#2. Begin with purpose. Everything makes sense in relation to purpose. When we lose sight of the purpose of anything, it stops making sense to us, we become confused, lose interest, and disengage.

So, let's explore the purpose of Advent and Christmas.

What is Christmas? Christmas is the Christian festival and season that celebrates the birth of Jesus. God sent His only son into the world to atone for humanity and restore our covenant and connection with God. It is a moment of singular importance in human history, one that has influenced all of human history for believers and non-believers since that first Christmas night.

The purpose of Christmas is to gratefully remember

who we are and all that God has done, is doing, and will continue to do for us.

What is Advent? Advent is the first season of the Christian calendar. The first Sunday of Advent is the New Year's Day of the Church's year. Advent is a time of preparation for the celebration of the birth of Jesus Christ at Christmas, and also a period of mindfulness and preparation for the Second Coming of Christ.

Preparation is a critical aspect of success. We prepare for everything we consider important in this life. So, if you want to have your Best Christmas Ever, preparation will be an essential component. The Church in her wisdom understands this and that is why Advent was established.

What is the purpose? What is the desired outcome? These are critical questions in preparing for anything.

The purpose of Advent is to prepare your soul to receive Jesus at Christmas in ever new and deeper ways. Keep this purpose ever in mind as you make your plans to prepare for Christmas. Everything will make sense or become senseless in relation to this purpose. If baking cookies helps you achieve this purpose, bake away. Sitting quietly on a park bench, taking long walks in quiet places, visiting your church each day, reading, singing, serving others... whatever it is that helps you achieve the purpose of Advent, give yourself to those activities.

Wake up each day with this purpose in your heart and on your mind. Purpose has a way of transforming the way we live our lives. Allow the purpose of Advent to transform you.

When he was President, Abraham Lincoln wrote to a friend, "Nothing will divert me from my purpose." Let that be your attitude as you journey toward Christmas this year. And as you know, there will be a great many people and things that will try to divert you from the true purpose of Advent and Christmas. Let nothing divert you from your purpose.

3.
Life is Short!

Any minute now we will all be dead. I know it's a bit morbid. But death provides context for life, and those who reflect on death for even just sixty seconds each day are significantly less likely to waste their lives.

#3. Reflect on the shortness of life. The Roman philosopher and statesman Seneca wrote, "Most mortals complain bitterly because we are born for a brief span of life." He went on to explain that life is shortest for those who waste it, and the brutal truth is that we have all invented our own intricately personalized ways to waste portions of our one short life.

Steve Jobs, co-founder of Apple Computers said in his commencement speech at Stanford, "For the past 33 years, I have looked in the mirror every morning and asked myself: If today was the last day of my life, would I want to do what I am about to do today? And whenever the answer has been 'No' for too many days in a row, I know I need to change something... almost everything. All external expectations, all pride, all fear of embarrassment or failure–these things just fall away in the face of death, leaving only what is truly important."

Life is short. You are dead an awful long time. What is truly important?

Think of it this way. What can you take with you from this life to the next? I don't mean things. Reflect on your day yesterday, on everything you did yesterday. What would you feel comfortable bringing with you to the next life and laying at the feet of God as an offering?

Do something today that you can take with you into eternity.

4.
The Main Thing.

What you choose to focus on is so important in life. It's important in your career, in your personal finances, with your health, in your marriage and parenting, in your spirituality, and in every other aspect of life.

Focus. This is one of the most powerful tools you possess. Whatever you choose to focus on will determine everything. This is true at every stage of life, and it is true during Advent and Christmas. Choose to focus on everything being perfect and you will drive yourself crazy and probably everyone else too. Choose to focus on everything being perfect and Christmas will be your most anxious and stressful day of your year.

Focus on Jesus and that will determine everything. As we journey toward Christmas, think of Peter getting out of the boat and walking on the water toward Jesus. He was walking on water, until he took his eyes off Jesus. Then he began to sink. The same is true for you and me.

Jesus is the main thing. Well, he is obviously not a thing, but in the context of keeping the main thing the main thing, you know what I mean. And if Jesus is the main thing, the color of the napkins is not the main thing. If everyone can come is not the main thing. What we eat is not the main thing. The perfect gift is not the main thing. Whether or not the Christmas tree is too large or small is not the main thing.

This Christmas, keep your eyes on Jesus. Keeping the main thing the main thing makes life a lot simpler, and with that simplicity comes lightheartedness... and lightheartedness is a sign of the spiritual childhood we should all aspire to experience at Christmas.

The wisdom of Margery Williams in
100th Anniversary Edition The Velveteen Rabbit
will help you develop that lightheartedness.

5. Temper Your Expectations.

Our expectations get us into a lot of trouble, especially those expectations that we keep to ourselves. They can be the source of so much misery and disappointment.

Welcome back to our exploration of twenty-eight ways to make this your Best Christmas Ever!

#5. Temper your expectations.

Sometimes lowering your expectations is the only sane thing to do. Every family has stories about people who do the same thing year after year to offend and upset others. Their actions are no doubt the primary problem, but you get to decide how you respond to their actions. And you get to set your own expectations.

The gap between what we expect to happen and what actually happens is where so much of our unhappiness resides. I call this the Expectations Gap. Five things fill the gap: disappointment, resentment, anger, frustration, and loss of trust.

Take some time to think about the expectations you have of other people this Christmas. Are they reasonable? Will they meet them? Do you need to adjust your expectations?

Then take some time to think about the expectations you have of yourself this Christmas. Are they reasonable? Will you meet them? Do you need to adjust your expectations?

And now, take some time to think about the expectations other people have of you this Christmas. Are they reasonable? Will you meet them? Do you need to have a conversation with anyone to adjust those expectations?

It might be time to reset some of your expectations.

6.
Create Memories.

What are your favorite Christmas memories? What do you remember about Christmas as a child? Probably not the things your parents were worried and anxious about. This realization helps us to prioritize what matters most, and remember that many of the things we worry about, nobody else notices.

#6. Create memories. Making memories is infinitely more important than giving gifts. So, as we journey toward Christmas, each time you think about giving someone a gift, reflect for a moment on your favorite memory with that person–it may be a Christmas memory, it probably isn't, and that's okay.

Dreams and memories are both powerful gifts God has given us. Spend some time dreaming and praying about the memories you want to create with and for others this Christmas.

If you are short of ideas, ask the people in your life

about their favorite Christmas memories. Ask friends and family. Ask strangers that cross your path over the next couple of weeks.

Hearing other people's favorite Christmas memories will bring new levels of clarity and intentionality to your preparations for Christmas this year.

Two things stand out for me in particular:

1. The vast majority of people's favorite Christmas memories have nothing to do with gifts, and yet we spend an inordinate amount of time, money, and energy focused on gifts at Christmas. People remember the intangibles: throwing snowballs, sitting by the fireplace, someone being able to make it home unexpectedly, going to Church, and the unmitigated joy of children. The best things in life are free. The most amazing and memorable aspects of Christmas don't cost anything. In fact, you cannot buy them with all the money in the world.

2. Many of the things we get all worked up about don't matter that much. So if you feel yourself getting anxious and stressed, ask yourself: Does this really matter? Is it important to another person, to God, or to my ego?

And don't forget to spend some time reflecting on

your fondest Christmas memories.

Christmas is a magical time to make memories with the people we love. Do it intentionally this year. If you are trying to pass your faith onto children or grandchildren, may I suggest intentionally creating some spiritual memories.

Mother Teresa's wisdom in
Do Something Beautiful for God
will teach you how to intentionally
create some spiritual memories.

7. The Power of Anticipation.

Growing up with my seven brothers in Australia, the anticipation that would build as we got closer to Christmas was epic. We would count how many "sleeps" we had until Christmas. The energy was electric. It was like watching pressure build to launch a rocket.

#7. Harness the power of anticipation.

In January each year I encourage team members to plan half their vacation time for the year. The reason? To harness the power of anticipation. Fifty percent of the benefits of a vacation come from anticipating it. When there are two feet of snow on the ground in February, and work is a bit overwhelming, knowing that you have a few days planned in a warm place come April changes the way you experience the pressure of work and the cold of winter.

When my father was dying of cancer, he would focus on the next event: a trip, the birth of a grandchild, or a family wedding. Those events became his focus instead of the treatment and were no doubt parts of what allowed him to live much longer than his doctors thought he would.

Anticipation is powerful. Tell your friends, children, spouse, and grandchildren what you are looking forward to experiencing with them this Christmas. You can help those around you experience Advent simply by saying, "I'm really looking forward to going to church with you on Christmas Day."

Harness the power of anticipation and put it to good use this Christmas.

8. Rediscover Childhood.

"Unless you change and become like children, you will never enter the kingdom of heaven." This was Jesus' counsel in the Gospel of Matthew (Matthew 18:3). Today we are going to explore what it means to become like children again.

#8. Rediscover childhood. Nobody experiences the unmitigated joy of Christmas like children.

Being a father has been an amazing blessing on my life. It has transformed me in unimaginable ways. Every day my children teach me new lessons. So, when I think about how we might rediscover childhood this Christmas, I am immediately drawn to two enduring lessons.

Play is the first. Children find a way to make everything a game. Gamification comes naturally to them. They run and laugh, hide and seek, sing and dance, and make everything into an adventurous game.

A couple of years ago, I was going through a very difficult and stressful situation and a friend said to me, "Find a way to have fun with it. Find a way to turn it into a game." At first the advice seemed bizarre given the nature of the situation. Then it seemed impossible. But I have done it. Not at every point along the way, but when I have been able to find a way to have fun with it, the burden of the situation has been significantly decreased.

Children know how to play. Do you? George Bernard Shaw wrote, "We don't stop playing because we grow old; we grow old because we stop playing."

The second lesson children teach us effortlessly is timelessness. They don't ask, "What time is it?" They live in the bliss of timelessness. They inhabit the eternal now, and revere the precious present.

So, this Christmas, put your watch away and make a point to play. To ease yourself into this renewed state of childhood, may I suggest you begin by reading some children's books.

9. Learn to Do Nothing.

This is a tough one for me. Learn to do nothing. I have spent my whole life trying to squeeze the most out of each day, each hour, each moment. But this obsession with efficiency often lures me away from what matters most.

#9. Learn to do nothing.

In the Fall of 1996, I read a book that continues to influence me to this day. It is one of a handful of books that I revisit every year. The book: Leisure: The Basis of Culture, by Josef Pieper with an introduction by T. S. Eliot.

It is a philosophical text and not easy to get through at times, but it holds profound insights of particular relevance to our modern lives.

What is leisure? Pieper provides the answer. Leisure is an attitude of mind and a condition of the soul that fosters a capacity to receive the reality of the world.

"Capacity to receive the reality of the world." Wow. How often do we turn away from the reality of a situation because it is too much? How often do we meet people in complete denial of reality in some aspect of their life?

The enemies of leisure are what Pieper calls "total work" (what we would call working all the time) and lives of distraction. Total work and constant distractions both prevent the deep reflection that leisure seeks to lead us into.

Leisure allows us to receive the gifts of wisdom, and discover that there is no amount of human effort that can attain this wisdom by itself. Leisure is therefore indispensable in our quest to thrive as human beings in this life and the next.

Why does leisure matter?

Piper points out that religion can only be authentically born in a person and society through leisure. It cannot be rushed. Leisure is indispensable for the contemplation of God. He also makes clear that leisure is the foundation of culture.

"Total work" makes wisdom, culture, religion, and contemplating God impossible. This is why "total work" was so central to Communism of the 20th century. Communism seeks to murder religion through "total work."

In our own place and time, it seems we are imposing the condition of "total work" upon ourselves.

Even when we're not doing paid work, we busy ourselves with all-manner of unpaid work that keeps us from the leisure that is essential to our human flourishing.

Psalm 48:10 counsels us, "Be still and know that I am God." Pieper translates it as, "Have leisure and know that I am God."

Have leisure and know God. Have leisure and grow in wisdom. Have leisure and grow to love more deeply. Have leisure and see the reality of the world as it really is.

Josef Pieper was a great philosopher. He was also a prophet. His work on leisure was written in 1948. With it he issued this stark warning, "Total labor vanquishes leisure. Unless we regain the art of silence and insight, the ability for nonactivity, unless we substitute true leisure for our hectic amusements, we will destroy our culture–and ourselves."

Paid and unpaid work of every type has only gobbled up more and more of our time since Pieper penned these words and the result has been exactly as he foresaw.

We have banished silence from our lives. We have replaced wisdom and insight with mere knowledge and information. Our amusements have only become more hectic. We have been seduced by endless distractions. We have destroyed culture and these things are destroying our very selves.

The hardest thing in the world to do is nothing. Leisure. Reflection. Basking in God's presence. This Christmas, learn to relax. Learn to do nothing. Establish leisure as part of your daily routine. And of course, what we discover when we start doing nothing is that leisure, true leisure, is anything but nothing. It's time to refuse the madness of rushing around.

10. The Santa Question.

Christmas is coming and so millions of children will ask their parents this question: Is Santa real? It's time we had a solid answer to the question.

#10. The Santa Question. Santa is Real. Just not in the way the world has distorted him.

The modern-day Santa that inhabits shopping malls is a distorted version of the life and example of a Saint Nicolaus. Nicolaus was born to a wealthy family in the third century. When his parents died, he distributed their wealth to the poor, became a priest, and became legendary for his profound generosity and care for people.

Stories spread far and wide about his generosity. The most famous incident from his life is the night he dropped a small sack of gold coins through the window into the house of a family in desperate need. This provided dowries for three daughters who would have otherwise almost certainly ended up being slaves or prostitutes.

By that time Nicolaus had become a bishop, and the father woke when he heard the sack being dropped through the window. Looking outside he caught a glimpse of the red and gold robes of the Nicolaus who had hoped to remain anonymous.

The father told everyone he knew about Nicolaus' generosity, and the beauty of anonymous giving was unleashed in the world. People everywhere began giving anonymously and the spirit and legend of Saint Nicolaus grew... and has continued to grow century after century... and lives on today!

Nicolaus is perhaps the inventor of anonymous giving. 1700 years after his death, his Spirit lives on as a confounding reminder of the obligation we have to those who live suffering on the brink of despair.

Is Santa real? Santa is most real not when we spoil our children with gifts, but when we teach them the spirit of Nicolaus by giving generosity to those most in need, bringing them a comfort and joy that we so often take for granted.

So, this Christmas, go out of your way to be the difference that makes all the difference for someone, somewhere. And together let's bring a little hope, comfort, and joy to those who need it more than we may ever need anything.

The generosity of God is staggering. May it live in you and me, more and more with every passing day.

Learn to astound the world with your generosity in ***The Generosity Habit.***

11.
Be a Pilgrim, Not a Tourist!

What is the difference between a pilgrim and a tourist? This is the question we will explore today.

#11. Be a pilgrim, not a tourist!

A pilgrimage is a sacred journey. For almost thirty years we have been hosting pilgrimages to the Holy Land; Fatima, Lourdes and Paris; Rome, Assisi, and Florence, and the Camino. On the opening night as we welcome the pilgrims, we always ask them the same question: Are you going to be a pilgrim or are you going to be a tourist?

Tourists want everything to go exactly as they have planned and imagined it. They rush around from one place to another making sure they cram everything in. They are constantly buying souvenirs and knickknacks, many of which they will look at when they get home and wonder, "What was I thinking?" Tourists get upset if there are delays. They demand prompt attention and service to their every need and desire. They focus on themselves, often shoving past others to get where they want to go. Tourists go sightseeing. Tourists count the cost.

Pilgrims are very different. They look for signs. If a flight gets delayed or canceled, they ask, "What is God trying to say to me?" Pilgrims are not concerned with seeing and doing everything, just the things they feel called to see and do. They are not obsessed with shopping. They are aware of the needs of others. Pilgrims go looking for meaning. Pilgrims count their blessings.

The reality is we are all pilgrims. This planet we call earth is not our home; we are just passing through. We build homes and establish ourselves here on earth in ways that ignore that we are really just here for a short time. It is a dangerous pastime to live as if you were never going to die, but consciously or subconsciously we all fall into this trap to various degrees.

We are only here on earth for the blink of an eye. This is not our home. That's why the happiness that God wants and created us for is very different from the fleeting happiness and momentary pleasures of this world. God created us for lasting happiness in a changing world and eternal happiness with him in heaven.

The happiness he wants for us in this life is a rare kind of happiness that is not dependent on situations or circumstances. It is easy to be happy when everything is going well. But Christian joy allows us to be happy like Paul was when he was in prison.

Do you ever think about heaven? It seems to me we don't talk about it anywhere near as much as we should. When Rudyard Kipling was very seriously ill a nurse asked him, "Is there anything you want?" He replied, "I want God!" We all do. We may not be aware of it, but we want God. Behind every desire for a new car or a new house, a promotion or accomplishment, clothes and jewelry, plastic surgery, adventure and travel, food and sex, acceptance and comfort, is our desire for God. We are always hungry for something more complete, and God is that completeness that we yearn for from the depths of our soul.

We are just passing through, and it is helpful to remind ourselves of that from time to time. In the context of eternity, we are only here for the blink of an eye. Realizing this changes our priorities. At the same time, we are here for a reason. You are here for a reason. God has a mission for you.

Life is a pilgrimage, a sacred journey. Typically, a pilgrimage is a journey to a religious shrine or a location important to a person's faith or beliefs. You can make a pilgrimage to the Holy Land, Rome, Fatima, Lourdes, the Camino, or any of the famous Christian sites around the world. But you could also make a pilgrimage to your nearest Cathedral. In fact, every Sunday you make a pilgrimage to your local parish for Mass.

Very often, people make pilgrimages with special intentions in mind. Some ask God for a favor, perhaps to heal a loved one who is sick. Others make a pilgrimage in thanksgiving for a blessing they have already received from God. There are always couples on our trips who are celebrating a wedding anniversary. They are making the trip to thank God for their marriage. On every trip, our priest chooses one of the holy places and invites every couple on the trip to renew their marriage vows. Powerful! I cannot even describe how powerful and moving this is. I have seen it many times, but still it moves me. Sometimes people make a pilgrimage seeking clarity on some decision they have to make.

Life is a pilgrimage, but sometimes you need a pilgrimage to discover life. We are journeying in this life toward the sacred city, toward the heart of God—heaven. Nobody makes the journey alone. We all need companions. Some of my very best friends in this world I met on pilgrimages. These trips that Dynamic Catholic hosts are life changing, and when you experience something like that with other people, you form a very special bond.

The best friends in the world encourage us and challenge us to become the-vest-version-of-ourselves, and by doing so, they help us to get to heaven.

Let us pray for the grace to be pilgrims and not just tourists. Let us pray for the grace to be the kind of friend who helps others in the great pilgrimage of life.

This is "A Pilgrim's Prayer," by Thomas Merton:

My Lord God,
I have no idea where I am going.
I do not see the road ahead of me.
I cannot know for certain where it will end...
Nor do I really know myself,
And the fact that I think I am following Your will
Does not mean that I am actually doing so.
But I believe that the desire to please You does in fact please You.
And I hope I have that desire in all that I am doing.
I hope that I will never do anything apart from that desire.

And I know that if I do this,

You will lead me by the right road, though I may know nothing about it.

Therefore I will trust You always though I may seem lost

And in the shadow of death.

I will not fear, for You are ever with me,

And You will never leave me to face my perils alone.

We are just passing through this place we call earth. At every turn we are tempted to be tourists, but we are pilgrims. Adopt the attitude of a pilgrim this Christmas.

12. Getting to Know Yourself.

How well do you really know yourself? This is the question we are going to explore today. Some of the benefits of an intimate knowledge of self are: less inner conflict, less conflict with others, compassion for others, fulfillment, joy, self-control, resistance to social pressures, and better life choices.

#12. Get to know yourself.

Both Plato and Socrates employed the phrase, "Know thyself." It is an invitation to self-exploration. But it is often met with a vagueness that leaves people not knowing where to start

or a narrowness that leaves people with a narrow sense of self. For example, it's great to know what your strengths are, but it isn't enough.

So, today, we are going to identify four specific ways to get to know yourself.

1. Values. What are your values? Without a clear

sense of our values our lives begin to drift.

2. Strengths and Weaknesses. Most people are delighted to look at their strengths, but actively avoid their weaknesses. And yet, it is often our weaknesses that hold the key to our bigger and better future.

3. Temperament and Personality. Take a personality assessment. There are many options. Read the assessment that your answers generate. Are they 100% accurate? No. Are they surprisingly insightful? Yes. Do they provide a great starting point for getting to know yourself? Absolutely.

4. Hopes and Dreams. We are driven by our dreams, consciously and unconsciously. What are your dreams? What are you doing about them? Are you pursuing them or neglecting them? Your dreams are your dreams for a reason.

5. Motives. Observe yourself. Ask yourself: Why am I doing this? There is a reason motive plays such a key role in the investigation of crimes. Motive reveals the light and darkness of the human heart. It is one of the fastest ways to know yourself if you can be brutally honest. The key is to realize our motive is almost never singular. We often have many entangled motives for any single decision or action.

As we journey toward Christmas, it's important to ask: What made Christmas necessary? The answer is messy and difficult to face. Our darkness made the light of Christmas necessary. How well do you know your own darkness? Not just the dark things you have done, but also, and perhaps more importantly, the dark things you are capable of. You may never do them, but the mere fact that you are capable of them is important self-knowledge.

Do you ever find yourself thinking or saying, "I would never do that!" This statement is almost never true. Given the same circumstances, the same mental disposition, the same fears or desperation, the same education and upbringing... you might find yourself doing exactly the same thing, or worse.

It's easy to know your goodness and strengths, but real self-knowledge often lay in getting to know our own darkness. But from this more complete sense of self will emerge a less judgmental, more accepting person whose heart is full of empathy and compassion for other people in their struggles.

Get to know yourself this Christmas and the role you played in making Christmas necessary.

13.
That Difficult Conversation.

Most of us need to have a difficult conversation with someone that we have been avoiding. What is that conversation for you? Who do you need to have it with? Don't carry that burden with you into Christmas and the New Year. The time to have that conversation is now.

#13. Have that difficult conversation.

How long have you been avoiding it for? How much stress, worry, and anxiety has that brought to your life? When should you have had the conversation? Is there a valid reason to put it off? And perhaps most importantly, how will you feel once you have this difficult but necessary conversation?

You have three options:

1. Continue to avoid the conversation and suffer the consequences,

2. Have the conversation in a clumsy and uninten-

tional way and suffer the consequences, or

3. Improve all the relationships in your life by learning how to have difficult conversations.

If option #3 is calling to you, the first step is to get clear about what you hope the conversation will accomplish. Do you simply need to be heard? Or is there an outcome you desire? This clarity will drive intentionality. It will also help you keep the conversation to its appropriate length. When difficult conversations are too long or too short, they tend to fail. The second step is to schedule the conversation at the right time and in the right place. The wrong time is when you are tired and distracted. The right place is where you can have a conversation without distractions and interruptions.

Have the difficult conversation you have been putting off before Christmas. It will help you have your Best Christmas Ever!

14. Escape the Joyless Urgency.

The joyless urgency of modern life is taking its toll on our health and relationships, on our spiritualty and morality. This year, step away from the joyless urgency that often even infects the way we experience and celebrate Christmas.

#14. Slow down.

The speed at which we do anything can change its meaning and outcomes. It is time to slow down and escape the joyless urgency that has gripped our lives.

To explore this lesson, let us consider the question: Does speeding get you there faster? A study conducted by the University of Sydney found that on average drivers saved just two minutes a week or 26 seconds per day.

Almost all theoretical gains are lost by unexpected delays. But even if you could travel at a constant speed of 75 miles per hour in a 55 mile per hour zone for 30 miles, you would only save 8.7 minutes. Is speeding worth it?

Take into account the costs of speeding, such as the stress and anxiety of getting a ticket, the increased chance of causing an accident, the possible financial penalties, and possible restrictions to your life if your license is revoked, and the obvious and not so obvious impact of all of these on your health, and it becomes clear that the risks far outweigh the reward.

And yet, we speed through life, joylessly.

Slow down as we journey toward Christmas. Slow down to the speed of goodness and generosity, patience and wisdom.

15. Listen to Music.

Music is one of the most amazing gifts life has to offer. A day without music is a day... I cannot even finish the sentence, for I cannot imagine. And while we may be tempted to dismiss a day without music as being easy to accomplish or of little consequence, this is only because we forget that music is everywhere.

Yes, music is everywhere, and because it is everywhere we have come to take it for granted. On elevators and in waiting rooms, at the supermarket and in restaurants, music is everywhere. But are we listening, or is it just blocking out other noise. I fear the latter, and what a soulless use of music that is.

#15. Listen to Music.

When was the last time you sat down and did nothing else but listen to music?

Take some time today to listen to music. Choose a song or an album. Let Mozart speak to you about the range of human experience or allow your favorite Christmas music to transport you to experience the mysteries of the divine intervention we call Christmas.

Find a quiet place, quiet your heart and mind, and listen to the music with new ears. Listen to the music as if you had never heard music before. Listen to the music as if you had been denied music for twenty years.

Learning to listen to music again will make your soul dance for joy.

16. Stop Trying to Hack Life.

The idea that life has to be hacked tells us all we need to know about our bankrupt culture. We have wandered so far from the purpose of life and so far into meaninglessness. The result is that we think we need to hack life, not to thrive, but merely to survive. It is time to stop trying to hack your life.

#16. Stop trying to hack your life.

Quick fixes don't work, short cuts defeat the purpose, and neither is a path to excellence.

Is there any such thing as a meaningful life hack? Is there any such thing as a profound life hack?

Life hacks are a distraction from the main event. Life is for living. Even our problems, frustrations, and inconveniences should be lived. Why? Because they serve the greater meaning and purpose of life, which is to help you grow in virtue and become the-best-version-of-yourself.

The fundamental mistake we make is to think that we are here to solve the problems. And yet, we know that as soon as we solve today's problem, another problem will emerge.

We are not here to solve the problems, the problems are here to solve us. When we work through problems with a values-based approach we grow in virtue. And virtue is the not-so-secret ingredient to improving as a human being, having a better life, and transforming society.

Our lives only genuinely improve when we grow in virtue. Society only authentically progresses when the people who make up that society grow in virtue.

Patience, kindness, compassion, generosity, courage... these are what we yearn for. These are the gifts to give those we love this Christmas.

17.
Learn to Deep Think.

Are you a lover of wisdom? The future of America and indeed humanity depends on enough people answering yes to this question.

The term philosopher is the combination of two Greek words. Philos, which means lover or friend. And Sophia, which means wisdom. Philosophy is therefore love of wisdom. A philosopher is a lover of wisdom or a friend to wisdom.

Mention philosophy and many people will think or say something like: "That's too deep for me." Wisdom isn't too deep for anyone. It's just the right depth for everyone. It meets us where we are on the journey and illumines the next step.

In our own way and according to our calling we should each aspire to be philosophers. We should each strive to become lovers of wisdom.

#17. Learn to deep think.

None of the problems we face as a society can be solved by shallow thought. There is no quick fix for them. They cannot be hacked. Our biggest problem is that we lack what is essential if we are to solve all our other problems. Namely virtue, and in particular patience.

The future of America, and indeed the future of humanity, depends on enough people becoming lovers of wisdom. If this is true, these futures depend on patience. Why patience? Because all deep thought requires patience, and all our problems will require deep thought to solve.

When was the last time you got beyond the sound bites and brief articles and really studied a topic, issue, or problem?

Pick one. Pick a topic, issue, or problem and study it deeply. This deep thought is the type of leisure Josef Pieper was talking about. It is soul refreshing and life-altering.

The world needs wisdom. More than that it needs wise people. You can't Google wisdom. Google has no wisdom. It has information and knowledge, but wisdom is truth lived. It cannot be transmitted by books and lectures alone. Wisdom is most potent and most transmissible when someone lives it.

Think deeply about something this Advent and Christmas season. Deep thought is a beautiful thing. It will bring you joy. The joy of getting clearer every day about what matters most and what doesn't matter at all. That clarity will inform your decisions, and every wise decision brings with it more joy.

18.
Pay Attention.

"Beware of what you become in pursuit of what you want." Lance Armstrong, Bernie Madoff, Barry Bonds, Al Capone, Judas. They stopped paying attention to who they were becoming. Who are you becoming? Are you paying attention?

Welcome back to our exploration of twenty-eight ways to make this your Best Christmas Ever!

#18. Pay attention to what is happening inside you and who you are becoming.

What do you want? Do you know? Are you clear? Focused? Obsessed? "Beware of what you become in pursuit of what you want." These are the words of Jim Rohn. I remember the first time I heard this quote and how powerfully it struck me.

We want what we want because we believe it will make us happy. But if we become someone we don't like in the process of getting what we want, all success and accomplishment is empty. There is no point becoming successful if you don't like who you are once you reach your goal.

Lance Armstrong and Barry Bonds got all the accolades, but did they like who they became in pursuit of what they wanted?

Bernie Madoff got all the money, but did he like who he became?

Pablo Escobar and Al Capone had all the power, but did they like who they became in order to get there and stay there?

Success, fame, money, accomplishments, possessions, power. These are all tiny external realities compared to the enormity of not liking the person you became in order to get them. Too many people achieve what they thought would make them happy only to discover they are unhappy with themselves.

Nothing external can cure inner unhappiness.

Beware. It is such a powerful word. It means to be on one's guard. We are on guard and wary of the things other people can do to us, but often it is the things we do to ourselves that cause the most harm.

Beware anything and anyone that entices you to compromise your virtue and values. It always begins with something small. Beware of situations that will require heroic virtue. Best not to test yourself in these ways. Beware of opportunities that cost more than money. Beware of pretending to be someone you are not. Beware of your own envy and covetousness.

Do you like who you have become? Do you like the person you are becoming? Are you setting off on an adventure to accomplish something?

"Beware of what you become in pursuit of what you want." Take time each day to check in. Pay attention to what is happening inside you and who you are becoming.

19. Be Present Not Preoccupied.

Do what you can, where you are, with what you've got. It seems simple, logical, and reasonable. But we spend so much of our time and energy trying to impact things we cannot impact.

#19. Be present not preoccupied.

Being preoccupied is one of the great curses of our age. Everyone has experienced someone preoccupied with their phone or preoccupied with themselves. Their preoccupation makes them unable to be present. Preoccupied is unavailable.

Of course, it is easy to recall times other people have been preoccupied. But when was the last time you were preoccupied?

Sometimes we can't focus on the current thing because we are thinking about the next thing, and sometimes we are still caught up in the last thing. But being preoccupied always prevents us from being present. And we can't have our best anything if we are not present.

Everything good begins with being present. Being present is empowering. Your power to do good, and be good, and unleash a tidal wave of goodness in this world is relinquished when you are preoccupied.

What's the answer? Be present... and do what you can, where you are, with what you've got.

20.
Locate Your Heart.

Where is your heart? When we sing the National Anthem, we place our right hand on the left side of our chest to symbolically place our hand on our heart, but is that where our heart is located? No. The heart is located in the center of our chest. This of course is all very literal, but knowing where your heart is located spiritually is today's topic.

#20. Locate your heart.

Follow your desire and you will locate your heart.

Next time you are reading the Bible replace the word heart with desire and see what you learn about yourself.

"Trust in the LORD with all your heart." Proverbs 3:5

Trust in the LORD with all your desire. Do your desires reveal that you trust God?

"Above all else, guard your heart, for everything you do flows from it." Proverbs 4:23

Above all else, guard your desire, for everything you

do flows from it. Are good things flowing from your desires?

"Give me your heart and let your eyes delight in my ways." Proverbs 23:26

Give me your desire and let your eyes delight in my ways. Are you willing to give God your desire? Do your desires delight in God's ways?

"Create in me a pure heart, O God, and renew a steadfast spirit within me." Psalm 51:10

Create in me a pure desire, O God, and renew a steadfast spirit within me. It is impossible to have a steadfast spirit unless we have control of our desires. Are you able to direct your desires?

"Lord, examine my heart." Psalms 26:2

"Lord, examine my desires. What would God find if he examined your desires?

"They had not understood... for their hearts were hardened." Mark 6:52

"They had not understood... for their desires were hardened." How would you describe your desires?

"For where your treasure is, there your heart will be also." Matthew 6:21

For where your treasure is, there your desire will be also. Where is your desire? Follow your desire and you will locate your heart. Find your treasure and you will locate your heart.

We live in a culture suggests that we should follow our desires unquestionably. The assumption is that every desire we have is good, and we all know from personal experience that that is not true.

We live in a culture that suggests that happiness is simply a matter of getting what you want. Again, the assumption is that we always want what is good, right, just, and noble, and we all know that is not true.

Happiness is not a matter of getting what you want, but a matter of wanting the right things. If we desire the wrong things, things that for whatever reason are wrong for us, no amount of those things will bring us happiness.

Desire is not something that just happens to us. We can master our desires. We can direct our desires, and with our desires we can direct our hearts, and with our hearts we can direct our lives.

Christmas is a good time to check up on your heart. Do you know what you desire? Are you desiring things that are good for you? It's time to locate your heart and if it has wandered off course, return it to the straight and narrow path of joy.

21. Amazing Sundays.

I want to help you make every Sunday for the rest of your life amazing. Wouldn't that be an amazing Christmas gift?

#21. Amazing Sundays.

4,160. That's how many Sundays most people get. And we waste them. We waste them being too busy. We waste them being hungover. We waste them being unintentional. We waste them letting the culture push us around. We waste them. And Sundays are too good to be wasted.

I missed so many Sundays travelling. It is one thing that I regret looking back on all my years on the road. And perhaps in the larger scheme of things it isn't a regret, but I certainly have a sense of loss when I reflect on it.

Sundays are beautiful, because Sunday is the Sabbath. The Sabbath is more than a day of rest. It is a day or rejuvenation, realignment, and renewal.

When was the last time you really experience Sabbath? How long has it been since you tasted the joy of the Sabbath? Think about it. The joy of the Sabbath. It may have been a while. It may have been a very long while.

My prayer for you this Christmas is that you rediscover the Sabbath.

Whatever good things you want to increase in your life, honor the sabbath and it shall be so. This is the secret power of the sabbath. I cannot explain it fully. But reflect upon what it is you most want to increase in your life: Do you want a relationship to improve? Do you want to become healthier? Do you want more success in your career? Do you want to be a better parent? Do you want less stress and anxiety? Do you want the quality of your friendships to improve?

Whatever it is. Whatever good things you want to increase in your life, honor the sabbath and it shall be so.

Rediscover Jesus
will help you do just that.

22. Attend to Your Spiritual Illness.

When was the last time you had a spiritual check-up? Most people see the wisdom of having an annual physical with their doctor, and yet most people go many, many years without having a spiritual check-up.

#22. Attend to your spiritual illness.

We live in an amoral society. What does it mean to be amoral? It means to be lacking a moral sense. It means to have no concern for whether behavior is morally right or wrong. It means to be unprincipled and unethical. We live in an amoral society and that should concern us a lot more than it does.

One reason we should be more concerned is because it is impossible to live in such an environment and not be impacted by it.

Think about it like this. The effects of secondhand cigarette smoke have now been extensively studied and discovered to be enormous.

The CDC now warns us that, "Exposure to secondhand smoke interferes with the normal functioning of the heart, blood, and vascular systems in ways that increase the risk of having a heart attack. Even brief exposure to secondhand smoke can damage the lining of blood vessels and cause blood platelets to become stickier."

We are living in a world where every type of vice is celebrated as a personal right. How is that affecting our souls?

We are breathing in the amorality of the times.

Or have we crossed another line? Are we living in an amoral society, or are we now living in an immoral society?

What's the difference? What does it mean to be immoral? Immoral is to intentionally and conscientiously go against what is good, true, right, just, virtuous and ethical.

We are breathing in the immorality of the times. With each breath, the paths of right and wrong become a little more blurred. With each breath, our hearts and minds begin to question and rationalize and justify our own wayward behaviors, however small at first.

But here's the real question: Do we have the courage

to face our own moral weaknesses and failures?

Attend to your spiritual illness. It is time to prioritize your spiritual health.

23. Technology Fasting.

Is your phone the first thing you reach for each morning? Is checking email the first work-related activity you do each day? Do you grab your phone to check something quickly and then find yourself engulfed by it for an hour or more? Do you reach for your phone every time you have a spare minute in line at the grocery store, at a stop light, in the waiting room at the doctor's office? How do you feel if you leave your phone behind at home or in the car? What emotions rise up in you in these situations? How would you feel if your spouse or best friend had access to your phone and was able to see and read everything?

#23. Technology fasting.

Is it possible to have a healthy long-term relationship with your phone, one that leaves you feeling good about yourself and the way you spend your time?

Is your phone making you smarter or dumber? Is

your phone bringing you relaxation and happiness or stress and anxiety? If your best friend was dating someone who made her feel the way your phone makes you feel, would advise your friend to break up with that person?

You might not need to break up with your phone, but you might need a break and a reset.

These questions only scrape the tip of the iceberg. The issues that technology has ushered into our lives are significant. But to understand just how significant, I propose a technology fast. One day, two days, or three days. You decide. No phone or computer. You will be amazed how difficult it is, and you will be astounded how differently you feel once you get over the withdrawal symptoms.

You will think more clearly. You will be more decisive and make better decisions. You will have better conversations. Your relationships will feel completely different.

It's time for a technology fast, or perhaps just a phone fast. You decide. By fasting you may realize that you need a new relationship with technology. You may decide you need new habits when it comes to your phone.

Just try it. Pick a time to start and finish and commit.

Our lives change when our habits change, and fasting brings clarity to our hearts and minds so that we can see what new habits we need.

This technology fast will change your life, transform your relationships, and help you to have your Best Christmas Ever!

24. The Importance of Christmas PJs.

God created you to flourish. Are you flourishing this year? As you look to Christmas are you confident that what you have planned is going to help you and those you love to flourish? If not, it is time to adjust the plan. It is time for some fun, healthy, serious, lighthearted, profound and bold routines, rituals, and traditions.

#24. Routines, rituals, and traditions.

Routines, rituals, and traditions play a powerful role in human flourishing. They can be as silly as Christmas pajamas or as profound as Midnight Mass.

The Kelly children love their Christmas PJs. It's a fun tradition. Does it have deep and profound meaning? Yes and no. On the surface it may seem like a silly materialistic tradition. But it is so much more than that.

As we journey toward Christmas, the season of Advent is a wonderful time to establish or reestablish some routines, rituals, and traditions. Make them healthy, bold, and playful.

Now, not every routine, ritual, and tradition can be all three. Christmas PJs can be fun and playful. Midnight Mass can be bold and profound. Taking a walk each day and praying for your family and friends as you walk can be bold, healthy, and playful.

Keep in mind that anything spiritual in the current cultural environment is bold. And boldness is good for the human spirit. Boldness stirs our souls and lets us know that our soul still has the vitality necessary to stand up for what is good, right, just, and noble.

This Christmas will change your life forever if you establish a new routine. What is the one thing you could do each day that would change everything for you? Why aren't you doing it? Ask God for the grace this Christmas to establish that as a routine in your life.

25.
The Sights, Smells, and Sounds of Christmas.

To have your Best Christmas Ever I am convinced that we have to engage all our physical senses... hearing, smell, taste, touch, and sight... and your spiritual senses... imagination, intuition, empathy, motivation, awareness, to name a few.

#25. The Sights, smells, and sounds of Christmas.

How do you experience Christmas through the sense of hearing? Think about your favorite sounds at Christmas: Christmas music, Church bells, children laughing, carolers singing, gifts being opened, the fire crackling...

How do you experience Christmas through the sense of smell? What does Christmas smell like for you? Apple pie, pecan pie, the smell of a fresh Christmas tree, incense at church, crisp cold fresh air, hot chocolate, gingerbread, an open fire, pudding, cinnamon...

How do you experience Christmas through the sense of sight? What does Christmas look like for you?

Stars, the Manger, reindeer, the child Jesus, nutcracker, snowflakes, a packed church, candles...

Now consider some of your spiritual senses...

How is God inviting you to engage your imagination this Christmas?

How is God inviting you to engage your intuition this Christmas?

How is God inviting you to a deeper empathy?

What area of your life is God calling you to engage your motivation?

How is everything you are doing this season increasing your awareness?

26. Movie Night.

"He's got the IQ of a rabbit."

"Yes, but he's got the faith of a child—simple."

This is part of the conversation that takes place between the angels at the beginning of the movie It's a Wonderful Life talking about George Bailey.

Have you ever been praised for having the faith of a child? Have you ever aspired to have the faith of a child?

#26. Movie night.

Have a movie night. Watch it alone or include everyone and anyone you wish. But pick a movie this year and commit to watching the same movie every Christmas for the rest of your life.

It is what is unchanging that allows you to make sense of the change. Fixed points of reference like the North Star allow us to navigate through life. And something as simple as a Christmas movie can help us assess our lives and provide clarity about what matters most and what matters least.

My Christmas movie, like millions of other people, is It's a Wonderful Life. We could have spent these twenty-eight days just exploring the lessons from this extraordinary film. We could spend 100 days exploring the lessons from this movie. Here are 21 lessons from It's a Wonderful Life.

1. George is the underdog. Mr. Potter is the top dog. We all underdogs and top dogs in different ways and at different times in our lives. How we deal with each of those scenarios determines the character of a person.

2. George loved people. He was the living embodiment of a man of the people and a man for the people.

3. We are all having an impact. George had no idea how much good he was doing. The angel Clarence said, "Each man's life touches so many other lives, and when he isn't around he leaves an awful hole, doesn't he?" We all forget our influence from time to time. In fact, most of us forget our influence most of the time it would seem to me.

4. George does at times feel sorry for himself. At one-point things get so bad that he says, "I wish I'd never been born." Are you feeling sorry for yourself

this Christmas?

5. Count your blessings. It is a simple, ancient path from discouragement and hopelessness to hope and the next step forward.

6. Poverty has a thousand faces, and we are all called to help the poor. But you cannot help the poor, whatever their poverty, from afar. We are each called to have a relationship with the poor. As Joseph the angel says, "If you're going to help a man, you want to know something about him, don't you?"

7. This is what the richest man in town had to say about the best man in town, "So, I suppose I should give [the money] to miserable failures like you and that idiot brother of yours to spend

for me." It is often the people who appear to be miserable failures and idiots who make the biggest impact in this world.

8. Your worldview effects the reality you experience. Do you remember the big, old house? "Oh, look at this wonderful old drafty house. Mary! Mary!" George Bailey says. Mary replies, "It's full of romance, that old place. I'd like to live in it." George was seeing the current state. Mary was envisioning the future state. George saw a house; Mary saw a home.

9. Prayers do get answered. Not always in the way you would like, but there is providence in that. As Garth Brooks notes, "Some of God's greatest gifts are unanswered prayers."

10. One of the clearest indicators of George Baileys character can be witnessed when his brother wins the Congressional Medal of Honor. He was happier that his brother won it than he would have been if he had won it himself. In a world that seems to be spiraling ever deeper into a pit of envy, let us never forget that the ability to delight in other people's successes, accomplishments, good luck, and blessings is a rare trait that should be fostered every chance we get.

11. George is always helping other people. When we help others, there is always something in it for us, and that's okay. It may be as simple as the warm feelings helping others fills our hearts with. Accept that, enjoy that, bask in that. The angel Clarence asks, "If I should accomplish this mission—I mean—might I perhaps win my wings?" He wanted to do good for others and he wanted good things for himself. And that's okay. But helping others requires sacrifice, sometimes dream crushing sacrifice. George was all too familiar with the cost of helping others, but he often overlooked

how helping others helped him, and was blind to how helping others had transformed him into a fine human being.

12. Life can be messy and difficult and disappointing. We hear the frustration of all this when George says, "Why did we have to live here in . . . this measly, crummy old town?"

13. Who is my neighbor? I think this may be the central question of the human experience. I'm not certain and I may see it differently in the future, but I have been pondering this for many years now, and what strikes me most is our desire to reduce the number of people we count as our neighbors. We have been doing it as human beings for thousands of years. This narrowing is an abdication of responsibility we have to our neighbor. It is never more starkly put than when the cranky, old, frustrated, unhappy, Mr. Potter says, "They're not my children" of the children who will be affected by his foreclosures.

14. George's dad was also a good man, a quiet achiever. Where are the quiet achievers in our social media addicted society? He is a man of perspective. He knows what matters most. He says to George, "You know, George, I feel that in a small way we are doing some-

thing important. Satisfying a fundamental need. It's deep in the race for a man to want his own roof and walls and fireplace, and we're helping him get those things in our 'shabby little office.'"

15. George was his father's son. His father was a fine man, and he became a fine man. There is a cause-and-effect relationship here that our culture seems to have forgotten. There is no substitute for a father with character who cares.

16. Stick together. "We can get through this thing all right. We've got to stick together, though. We've got to have faith in each other," is what George says as he is rallying the town to avoid disaster.

17. George was always looking for the best in people, not the good, the best.

18. We all have moments of desperation. George says to Clarence the angel, "Help me, Clarence. Get me back . . . Please, God, let me live again." It would seem to me that we all need to learn how to live again, and that there is no better time of year to do that than at Christmas.

19. George wanted to live a remarkable life, an extraordinary life. He wanted to do something truly unequivocal. When he was confused about what mattered

most, he thought his life was painfully ordinary. But the reality is his painfully ordinary life was extraordinary, remarkable, and unequivocal.

20. Sometimes the richest people have the least money.

21. Success often comes disguised as failure and the critics almost never know what they are talking about. In 1946, when It's a Wonderful Life was released, it failed at the box office, it was thrashed by reviewers, and it didn't win any Academy Awards. "So mincing as to border on baby talk," wrote the New Yorker. "For all its characteristic humors, Mr. Capra's Wonderful Life . . . is a figment of simple Pollyanna platitudes," wrote the New York Times. The company that produced it lost a fortune and went into liquidation. Both success and failure are illusions, and we should never let our critics direct our lives.

"He's got the IQ of a rabbit."

"Yes, but he's got the faith of a child—simple."

This Christmas lets us all aspire to the simple faith of a child.

27. Acceptance and Surrender.

Christmas is almost here. Are you prepared? You have prepared for the expected, now it's time to talk about the unexpected. The unexpected is inevitable. We may not know what form it will come in, but we know our plans will be derailed or diverted at some point. How we respond in those moments can make all the difference. Will you wrestle with reality and try to control the uncontrollable, or will you accept and surrender to the moment.

Today I am going to give you four words that will change those moments forever.

#27. Acceptance and surrender.

Expect the unexpected. And when it rears its sometimes ugly head, acceptance and surrender are your friends.

Accept your relatives as they are. They probably mean well and are doing the best they can with their current level of knowledge, awareness, and understanding. Try to have fun with the unexpected. Enjoy their eccentricities. Surrender to the moment. Don't try to control. Don't give it more meaning than it deserves. Much of what people do and say is caught up in the trivialities of life, so don't get all worked up. Accept where they are in their journey, trust that God is inviting them to take one step closer to Him today, and try not to be an obstacle to them taking that one step closer to God. Accept. Surrender. Make this a judgement free Christmas.

How? I know it's easy to talk about, but in the moment, it can be incredibly difficult to do. Our families know exactly how to push all our buttons. There is a very simple reason for that. They installed them. So, they know exactly where they are.

But here are the four words that will change everything.

Trust. Surrender. Believe. Receive.

Trust that God has this moment in the palm of His hand, and that there is no better place to be than in the palm of His hand.

Surrender. Stop resisting what is unimportant and inevitable. Let it be.

Believe that this moment is unfolding for some purpose unrevealed to you in this moment.

Receive. Open yourself to receiving every blessing God wants to fill you with. Open yourself to peace, surrender, acceptance, and the joy of the moment.

Trust. Surrender. Believe. Receive.

Trust. Surrender. Believe. Receive.

Trust. Surrender. Believe. Receive.

Say these words over and over again this Christmas, especially during the difficult moments created by difficult people. Trust. Surrender. Believe. Receive.

You may also enjoy
The Fourth Quarter of Your Life: Embracing What Matters Most.

28.
Everyone Knows that Love is the Only Way.

Do you have a big heart? Some people have huge hearts. They seem to have enough love, compassion, generosity, and empathy for everyone who crosses their path. Have you ever thought about increasing your heart size? Love like never before this Christmas. Set out to grow your heart three sizes this year.

#28. Everyone knows that love is the only way.

James Taylor is one of the great singer songwriters of the past 100 years. He was discovered by none other than the Beatles and was the first artist to record with the Beatles record label.

His lyrics are brilliant in their ability to capture ordinary life and entwine it with profound insights into the human experience and spirit.

"The secret of life is enjoying the passage of time.

Any fool can do it, there ain't nothing to it...

"The secret of love is in opening up your heart.

It's okay to feel afraid, but don't let that stand in your way...

Everyone knows that love is the only way. It's true. It's true on two counts. It's true that love is the only way, and it's true that everyone knows that. We forget it, ignore it, avoid it, neglect it, and get entangled in our selfishness, but somewhere deep inside we know that love is the one true path.

Christmas is an epic moment of love. It is the moment when history stood still and out of infinite love God came into the world and placed himself right in the middle of our mess.

The mess was vast. The mess is vast. It is caused when we choose some path other than love.

We all have love wounds. If we are going to love more than ever before we might need to explore our love wounds. Love lost. Love withheld. Love betrayed. Love neglected.

What did you have to do to receive love as a child?

What conditions do you place on your love?

What do your friends, children, spouse, partner have to do to receive your love?

The real magic of Christmas is God's love.

It is found in that peaceful moment of connection

with God...

The tender carefree timelessness with family...

The laughter of a family around the dinner table...

The sheer excitement and delight of children rushing to the tree Christmas morning in search of their gifts...

It is found in one neighbor's concern for another...

and in the feeling of rejuvenation that settles into your soul through the giving and receiving of unconditional love.

This Christmas grow your heart three sizes. Allow God to fill your heart with love and joy, generosity and hope. Speak your love. Speak it again. If you struggle to speak your love, write a note, or write a letter. Do not let Christmas pass without letting the people you love know just how much you love them.

Go into this Christmas season as if it were your last. Make it your Best Christmas Ever by treasuring it as if it were your last. Death puts life in perspective. If you knew you were going to depart this life before next Christmas, what would you make sure you did this Christmas?

29.
Holy Moments.

Merry Christmas!

My hope and prayer for you this Christmas is Holy Moments. May your life be filled with Holy Moments, and together may we fill our country with Holy Moments.

Some moments are holy, some moments are unholy, and we get to decide.

When I look at the world and I look at our country, it seems there is so much division and vitriol. What will deliver us from this moment in history? Holy Moments.

It is time to unleash a tidal wave of goodness. It is time to set in motion a domino effect of Holy Moments.

So, this Christmas I invite you to join the Holy Moments movement.

You have so much more to offer. You sense it. You may have known it for a long time. It's a truth that lingers, waiting patiently for us to pay attention to it. It's a soul sense, and when your soul senses such a thing, it should never be ignored.

When you sense that something is missing, that there must be more to life, or that you have so much more to offer, your intuition has never been so sharp. Claim these as sacred truths about yourself. Listen and follow where they lead.

We crave more because we were made for more. We try to satisfy those cravings with trivial activity and meaningless things. But this foolishness just leaves us exhausted, dissatisfied, and hungrier than ever.

Knowing what you hunger for is wisdom.

Some moments are holy, some moments are unholy, and our choices can guide a moment in either direction.

Holy Moments give meaning and divine purpose to our lives. Meaning is crucial to our health and happiness. We cannot thrive as human beings without it.

Holy Moments solve the meaninglessness of our lives.

There is a moment at the end of each day, when we lay our head on our pillows. Our bodies are tired, our minds relax, and our egos let go. It is a solitary moment. If we listen carefully in that moment, we will discover where we stand. That moment never lies. It reveals the meaning or meaninglessness of our lives.

Our ability to guide moments toward what is holy demonstrates that each and every human act contains profound meaning.

Our choices are at the heart of our ability to collaborate with God to create Holy Moments.

If you only learn to master one moment in your life, learn to master the moment of decision.

We all make choices. That's the easy part. The hard thing about choices is living with them.

Make choices that are easy to live with. Make choices you can look back on longingly, like you do upon the best of times with the best of friends.

The wisdom of Holy Moments will teach you how to become a great decision maker.

When you have a decision to make, consult your future self. Imagine yourself twenty years from now, looking back on this moment, and honor what your future self advises you to do.

When we teach children that choices have consequences, the emphasis is usually placed on the consequences of poor choices, while the powerful and positive consequences of wise choices are often overlooked.

Holy Moments are choices with powerful and positive consequences. Holy Moments are choices that are easy to live with.

If you are ready for a change, it only takes a handful of Holy Moments to flood your soul with joy and show you a new and exciting vision of the rest of your life.

Each Holy Moment is a mini-transfiguration. Holy Moments allow us to see what is possible, even if only for a fleeting moment. Each Holy Moment reveals who you are capable of being, and who you are capable of being is amazing.

The rest of your life is waiting for you. So, don't let your past rob you of your future. You are more than the worst thing that has ever happened to you. You are more than the worst thing you have ever done. God is never more than one choice away. It only takes one Holy Moment to shift the momentum of your life in the right direction.

Holy Moments make us better husbands and wives, parents and children, friends and neighbors, brothers and sisters, colleagues and citizens. Holy Moments make us better human beings.

Holy Moments remind us that the future can be better than the past. They fill us with hope. They show us that we have a vital role to play in bringing about that better future.

Holy Moments empower us to give others the gift of hope, and the ability to give other people hope is profoundly beautiful. Anything that can bring people hope is of infinite value. Holy Moments are such a thing.

Every unholy moment makes us less of who we were created to be, and every unholy moment makes the world a little more of a mess. When we abandon our destiny, we harm ourselves and others, make happiness impossible, and leave behind us a trail of collateral damage.

Holy Moments are the solution to the world's problems. This great collaboration between God and humanity is the untested solution to our problems. Unholy moments got us into this mess and only Holy Moments will get us out of it.

The culture's aggression toward morality and dismissal of anything spiritual will be the major obstacles to progress in society from this moment onward.

You cannot improve your life in any meaningful way without improving as a human being. And what is true for one person is true for an entire society. Virtue acquired one Holy Moment at a time is the only way for a society to make genuine progress.

Spirituality provides the tools necessary to develop empathy, temperament, impulse control, sustainable relationships, social responsibility, authentic leadership, and problem-solving skills.

It is time to stop searching for worldly solutions to spiritual problems.

My dream is to unleash a massive tidal wave of Holy Moments by raising up an amazing grassroots movement to transform our culture one Holy Moment at a time.

You were made in the image of God. Act accordingly!

The soul-expanding concept of Holy Moments is a breath of fresh air in a world polluted by so many soul-diminishing ideas and experiences.

Are you living a life of focus or distraction? What distractions have taken your life off course? What distractions are trying to lure you to your doom? Do you believe a life of focus would be more fulfilling than a life of distraction?

We are all confronted, sooner or later, with two of life's quintessential questions: Are you satisfied with your life? Are you satisfied with the direction the world is moving in?

Too often we are bold when we should be timid, and timid when we should be bold. Holy Moments require boldness.

"Be bold and mighty forces will come to your aid," was Goethe's counsel. I pray that Christmas stirs up your boldness.

Christmas is a Holy Moment like no other. But the spirit of Christmas longs to live in us all, if we will but soften our hearts and invite it in. And more than that, Christmas is an invitation to share God and His goodness with everyone who crosses our paths... one Holy Moment at a time.

Some moments are holy, some moments are unholy, and you get to decide. Fill your life and the world with Holy Moments!

Merry Christmas! May your Christmas be filled with Holy Moments... I pray this Christmas season inspires you to look for opportunities to create and encourage Holy Moments every day for the rest of your life.

Request your free copies of
Holy Moments: A Handbook for the Rest of Your Life
by visiting HolyMomentsBook.com

We wish you a Merry Christma

nd a Happy New Year!

nd a Happy New Year!

We wish you a Merry Christma

Worst Christmas Ever

28 Things That Will Prevent You from Having Your Best Christmas Ever!

Matthew Kelly

Published by Blue Sparrow
An Imprint of Viident

To learn more about the author, visit:
MatthewKelly.com

ISBN: 978-1-63582-531-2 (softcover)

Designed by Todd Detering

10 9 8 7 6 5 4 3 2 1

FIRST EDITION

Printed in the United States of America

Table of Contents

1. Fear of Missing Out. 1
2. Lack of Purpose. 3
3. No Plan. 4
4. The Wrong Content. 5
5. Taking Things Personally That are Not Personal. 7
6. Technology. 8
7. Superficiality. 9
8. Non-essentials. 10
9. Lack of Reflection. 11
10. Head Trash. 12
11. Materialism. 14
12. All the Rushing Around. 15
13. Not Asking for Help. 17
14. Procrastination. 18
15. Spending More Money than You Can Afford. 19
16. The Inability to Say No. 21
17. Unholy Moments. 22
18. Distractions. 24
19. Stagnation. 26
20. Lack of Boundaries. 28

21. Perfectionism. 29

22. The Inability to Let it Be. 31

23. Gluttony. 33

24. Living for the Wrong Audience. 35

25. Choosing to Be Right Rather Than Happy. 37

26. Negativity. 38

27. Ego. 40

28. Fear of Being Different. 42

1. Fear of Missing Out.

It's harder than you might think to have a great Christmas, and it's much easier to ruin your Christmas than it is to create your Best Christmas Ever.

There are of course plenty of very obvious ways to ruin Christmas for yourself and everyone around you. Examples include:

Insist on talking about politics.

Tell your relatives what you really think about them as if it were objective fact.

Re-wrap a gift someone gave you last year and regift it to the same person who gave it to you.

Try to control everything and everyone.

Tell every kid you meet that Santa isn't real and that their parents are lying to them.

There are the obvious ways... but we are going to explore the more subtle ways we sabotage our own Christmas experience and rob others of Christmas joy.

Obstacle #1 is: FOMO. Fear of missing out.

This is one of the greatest pieces of modern insanity. FOMO. The reality is you miss out on almost everything. The important thing is not to miss out on the things God created and intended just for you.

Focus on what matters most and don't worry about what you may or may not miss out on. If you focus on what matters most, what you miss out on is irrelevant. So get clear about what matters most.

Find your joy. Guard your joy. Follow your joy. Not just happiness. It seems our culture has confused happiness with comfort, and following comfort will lead you to misery. Find your joy. Cherish your joy. Guard your joy. And follow your joy.

2.
Lack of Purpose.

It's not easy to have a great Christmas in a world where everyone is striving for what isn't worth having.

Obstacle #2 is: Lack of purpose.

If you are unclear about the purpose of Christmas it will be impossible to have your best ever. So, take some time over the next couple of weeks to get clear about the purpose of Christmas.

This Christmas... Find your joy. Cherish your joy. Guard your joy. And follow your joy.

3.
No Plan.

It's not easy to have a great Christmas in a world where everyone is striving for what isn't worth having.

Obstacle #3 is: No plan.

Not having a plan will make it all but impossible to have a great Christmas. "Those who fail to plan can plan to fail," was Napoleon's counsel. You are not simply going to stumble into your Best Christmas Ever. It requires a plan and intentionality.

This Christmas... Find your joy. Cherish your joy. Guard your joy. And follow your joy

4. The Wrong Content.

It's not easy to have a great Christmas in a world where everyone is striving for what isn't worth having.

Welcome back to twenty-eight obstacles that will prevent you from having your Best Christmas Ever.

Obstacle #4 is: The wrong content.

The content you consume has an enormous impact on your life, your relationships, and your soul. Are the movies and shows you watch, the things you read, the music you listen to, and the conversations you have helping you become the-best-version-of-yourself? If not, they are dragging you down and they will be an obstacle to having your Best Christmas Ever.

Pay attention to the content you choose to consume between now and Christmas. I used to say we become the books we read, and it is still true. But we are also becoming the TV shows we watch. Look around society and you will see that this is true.

This Christmas... Find your joy. Cherish your joy. Guard your joy. And follow your joy.

5. Taking Things Personally That are Not Personal.

It's not easy to have a great Christmas in a world where everyone is striving for what isn't worth having.

Obstacle #5 is: Taking things personally that are not personal.

People do crazy things. People say crazy things. Don't try to understand them because they are often not reasonable or rational. And don't take them personally. Most people are too busy thinking about themselves to think about you, so don't inject their selfishness with meaning. Taking things personally that are not personal is a sure way to ruin Christmas.

This Christmas... Find your joy. Cherish your joy. Guard your joy. And follow your joy.

6.
Technology.

It's not easy to have a great Christmas in a world where everyone is striving for what isn't worth having.

Obstacle #6 is: Technology.

When you are dreaming of a fabulous Christmas you probably don't envision everyone sitting around the dinner table with their phones... but that is likely to happen unless you decide to do something about it. What if you agreed to make Christmas day a phone free day? Would that increase your chance of having an amazing Christmas?

Technology can be a real obstacle to having your Best Christmas Ever. Technology is great unless we become enslaved to it. Is your technology bringing you joy or sapping your joy?

This Christmas... Find your joy. Cherish your joy. Guard your joy. And follow your joy.

7.
Superficiality.

It's not easy to have a great Christmas in a world where everyone is striving for what isn't worth having.

We are continuing to explore twenty-eight obstacles that will prevent you from having your Best Christmas Ever.

Obstacle #7 is: Superficiality.

Superficiality is destroying our culture and our souls. Don't be afraid of the serious. Don't be afraid of deep thought. A bit of serious reflection is deeply agreeable to the human spirit.

Make a point not just to have small talk. Have some real conversations this Christmas. Watch a documentary. Read a book. Study an issue. Escape the superficiality that is an obstacle to having your Best Christmas Ever.

This Christmas... Find your joy. Cherish your joy. Guard your joy. And follow your joy.

8. Non-essentials.

It's not easy to have a great Christmas in a world where everyone is striving for what isn't worth having.

Obstacle #8 is: Non-essentials.

The tyranny of the many in this world of unlimited opportunities and possibilities is overwhelming us and exhausting us. The burden of all the non-essential nonsense will destroy your Christmas. Identify what is essential and focus on that.

Liberation is to be found in the vital few. Those few things that really matter.

This Christmas... Find your joy. Cherish your joy. Guard your joy. And follow your joy.

9.
Lack of Reflection.

It's not easy to have a great Christmas in a world where everyone is striving for what isn't worth having.

Obstacle #9 is: Lack of reflection.

Without time in the classroom of silence you will either go insane or at least begin to doubt your sanity in today's culture. We need time to reflect on what matters most if we are going to honor and celebrate it in our lives.

Establish a daily check in. A time of Christmas reflection to ask yourself: am I honoring my Christmas priorities? Am I focusing on what is essential? Or am I being carried away by the spirit of the world's superficiality?

This Christmas... Find your joy. Cherish your joy. Guard your joy. And follow your joy.

10.
Head Trash.

It's not easy to have a great Christmas in a world where everyone is striving for what isn't worth having.

Obstacle #10 is: Head Trash.

What is Head Trash? Head Trash is a collection of negative thoughts, self-defeating mind habits, and any other thoughts that take you away from the here and now. Head Trash leads you into self-limiting patterns of behavior such as: self-criticism, control, insecurity, judging self and others, procrastination, arrogance, paranoia, anger, fear, and unresolved guilt.

Sometimes we deposit this trash in our minds and sometimes other people deposit it in our heads. You may have Head Trash that has been there most of your life, and Head Trash that you collected today. Either way, as you prepare for Christmas this year, it's time to take out the trash.

This Christmas... Find your joy. Cherish your joy. Guard your joy. And follow your joy.

11.
Materialism.

It's not easy to have a great Christmas in a world where everyone is striving for what isn't worth having.

Obstacle #11 is: Materialism.

Materialism will destroy your Christmas. Things are great. Gifts are wonderful. But getting caught up in the material can block the spiritual reality which is of primary importance.

Materialism can also lead us down the toxic path of comparisons, especially in a culture obsessed with pretending and displaying the pretending on social media every minute of the day. Both materialism and comparing ourselves to others leaves us feeling empty.

This Christmas... Find your joy. Cherish your joy. Guard your joy. And follow your joy.

12. All the Rushing Around.

It's not easy to have a great Christmas in a world where everyone is striving for what isn't worth having.

Obstacle #12 is: All the rushing around.

Slow down. All the rushing around is a direct impediment to having your Best Christmas Ever. How do you know if you are moving too fast? If you wouldn't notice and enjoy the kiss of a snowflake on your cheek you are probably moving too fast.

Speed increases the chances of collisions and accidents. Not a good idea when driving and even more true when it comes to your life. Speed increases the chances that you will hurt yourself and hurt other people. Slow down as Christmas approaches. Make an active and intentional effort to slow your roll and be present to what is happening within you and around you.

This Christmas... Find your joy. Cherish your joy. Guard your joy. And follow your joy.

13. Not Asking for Help.

It's not easy to have a great Christmas in a world where everyone is striving for what isn't worth having.

We are exploring twenty-eight obstacles that will prevent you from having your Best Christmas Ever.

Obstacle #13 is: Not asking for help.

The people around you cannot read your mind. Let them know you need help, and most people will help if they are able to. Pretending you have everything handled when you're actually stressed and anxious isn't good for you, and it robs other people of the joy that comes from helping.

Not asking for help is an obstacle to having a fabulous Christmas, so this year, get really good at asking for help.

This Christmas... Find your joy. Cherish your joy. Guard your joy. And follow your joy.

14. Procrastination.

It's not easy to have a great Christmas in a world where everyone is striving for what isn't worth having.

Obstacle #14 is: Procrastination.

Procrastination is one of the great slayers of people's hopes and dreams, and it will slay your Christmas experience if you let it.

Procrastination is the arrogant assumption that God owes you another opportunity to do what you already had time to do.

Interestingly, feeling overwhelmed is one of the main reasons people procrastinate. You have enough time to do each day what God intends you to do that day, if you feel overwhelmed, look for the time wasters that are not part of God's plan for your day.

This Christmas... Find your joy. Cherish your joy. Guard your joy. And follow your joy.

15. Spending More Money than You Can Afford.

It's not easy to have a great Christmas in a world where everyone is striving for what isn't worth having.

Obstacle #15 is: Spending more money than you can afford.

It's hard to relax and enjoy anything when you are suffering from financial stress and anxiety. That increases when it is self-inflicted and unnecessary, caused by discretionary spending rather than necessities, because then we tend to add guilt and shame to the stress and anxiety.

Have a budget and stick to the budget. If you are tempted to go over your budget, use it as an opportunity to grow spiritually. Ask yourself: Am I tempted to spend more based on need or ego? What emptiness am I trying to fill by buying things? Am I aware that nothing external will fill the emptiness I experience within?

Spending more money than you can afford is an

obstacle to having a great Christmas. If you are short of cash this Christmas, search The Generosity Habit for ideas on how to be staggeringly generous without spending money.

This Christmas... Find your joy. Cherish your joy. Guard your joy. And follow your joy.

16.
The Inability to Say No.

It's not easy to have a great Christmas in a world where everyone is striving for what isn't worth having.

Obstacle #16 is: The inability to say no.

Learning to say no is one of the quintessential life skills in a world full of options. Sometimes the inability to say no is caused by overcommitment and often it is caused by lack of clarity. Get clear about what matters most this Christmas and you will get good at saying no to those things that don't matter.

Think before you say yes. As my good and wise father used to say, "Engage brain before opening mouth." Saying yes to the wrong things or too many things is an obstacle to having your Best Christmas Ever.

This Christmas... Find your joy. Cherish your joy. Guard your joy. And follow your joy.

17.
Unholy Moments.

It's not easy to have a great Christmas in a world where everyone is striving for what isn't worth having.

Obstacle #17 is: Unholy Moments.

Three in particular. When people come together there is always a temptation toward three types of unholy moments. Gossip. Judgement. Envy.

Gossip is character assassination, a type of spiritual murder. It poisons our souls and can quietly destroy a person's reputation, robbing them of future possibilities.

Judgement is stealing from God. Only God can see all things, know all things, and therefore judge something for what it really is. Our limited view means we almost never judge accurately.

Envy is ingratitude to God. It is denial of God's providence. It is basically saying to God, "You haven't given me enough." "I don't like what you have given me."

Don't let the poisons of gossip, judgement, and envy destroy your Christmas this year. Rise above.

This Christmas... Find your joy. Cherish your joy. Guard your joy. And follow your joy.

18.
Distractions.

It's not easy to have a great Christmas in a world where everyone is striving for what isn't worth having.

We are exploring twenty-eight obstacles that will prevent you from having your Best Christmas Ever.

Obstacle #18 is: Distractions.

What matters most should never be at the mercy of what matters least. But we live in a world of constant distraction. Unless you make a vigilant effort to stay focused on what matters most this Christmas, you will almost certainly get distracted.

How are you going to stay focused this Christmas? The ability to focus is one of your superpowers. What you choose to focus on has an enormous impact on your life. And allowing others to determine what you focus on is dangerous.

This Christmas... Find your joy. Cherish your joy. Guard your joy. And follow your joy.

19. Stagnation.

It's not easy to have a great Christmas in a world where everyone is striving for what isn't worth having.

Obstacle #19 is: Stagnation.

Stagnation is by definition lack of activity, growth, or development, the state of not flowing or moving. There are lots of ways this can enter and impact our life. You may be experiencing spiritual stagnation. You may be experiencing stagnation in your primary relationship. You may be experiencing financial or professional stagnation. And you may be experiencing social stagnation.

Stagnation is an obstacle to making this your Best Christmas Ever. So, identify the stagnation in your life and come up with a plan to get moving in that area of your life again.

This Christmas... Find your joy. Cherish your joy. Guard your joy. And follow your joy

20. Lack of Boundaries.

It's not easy to have a great Christmas in a world where everyone is striving for what isn't worth having.

Obstacle #20 is: Lack of boundaries.

Healthy emotional and psychological boundaries are essential to having a great Christmas. Here is a simple test to see if your boundaries are about to be violated: Do you feel free to say no? If not, why not? If you are not free to say no, you are not free to say yes.

One way people violate our boundaries all the time is by stealing our time. If people stole your money the way they steal your time, you would call the police. Guard your time this Christmas. Give it to the people and experiences that you feel called to give your time to.

And remember... Find your joy. Cherish your joy. Guard your joy. And follow your joy.

21. Perfectionism.

It's not easy to have a great Christmas in a world where everyone is striving for what isn't worth having.

Obstacle #21 is: Perfectionism.

You can have your Best Christmas Ever without having a perfect Christmas. There is no such thing as a perfect Christmas. So let that go right now.

Perfectionism is unrealistic and unhealthy. It often leads to anxiety, depression, and paralyzing inaction. It focuses on the outcome rather than the experience, and this usually leads us to miss out on the experience. Perfectionism is often an attempt to control something because we feel out of control personally. Many people will name perfectionism as a strength in job interviews, but in fact it is a weakness, and can actually become a disease. And, finally, perfectionism is a choice. So, choose a new approach this Christmas.

This Christmas... Find your joy. Cherish your joy.

Guard your joy. And follow your joy.

22. The Inability to Let it Be.

It's not easy to have a great Christmas in a world where everyone is striving for what isn't worth having.

Obstacle #22 is: The inability to let it be.

When people say, "Let it go!" they are basically saying stop thinking about it. But actively trying to stop thinking about something is impossible. Sometimes you can't let things go, at least not yet, and that's okay. You can't force your heart and mind to let things go. When you try to force this dynamic, these thoughts or memories tend to become more dominant, and you accomplish the reverse of your desired outcome. Trying to force yourself to let it go never works.

Letting it be is different. To let it be means to leave it alone. Like a mosquito bite, it may be irritating you, but leave it alone, just let it be. It won't change anything, but you won't waste endless amounts of time and effort on a hopeless situation or a situation that

you cannot influence regardless of what you do. Let it be means you won't waste your mental and emotional energy on a situation that you cannot change.

Let it be this Christmas. You know what your "it" is, but whatever it is, just let it be. It will help you and those you love to have an amazing Christmas.

And remember... Find your joy. Cherish your joy. Guard your joy. And follow your joy.

23. Gluttony.

It's not easy to have a great Christmas in a world where everyone is striving for what isn't worth having.

Obstacle #23 is: Gluttony.

Over the next month there will be so much food and drink on offer. Enjoy but don't overindulge. Overindulging robs you of joy. Overindulging turns pleasure into discomfort and pain. Not just physical pleasure and pain, but emotional pleasure and pain, psychological pleasure and pain, and spiritual pleasure and pain.

When we overindulge the head trash gets talking to us, and those voices lead us to places of disappointment, unhappiness, and self-loathing. Indulge by all means. Christmas is a feast to be enjoyed. To indulge means to allow yourself to experience and enjoy the pleasure. Indulge, just we wary of overindulging.

This Christmas... Find your joy. Cherish your joy. Guard your joy. And follow your joy.

24. Living for the Wrong Audience.

It's not easy to have a great Christmas in a world where everyone is striving for what isn't worth having.

Obstacle #24 is: Living for the wrong audience.

Trying to please the wrong audience will certainly prevent you from having your Best Christmas Ever. We should live our lives for an audience of one and let the rest of the chips fall where they may. The world will tell you that that audience of one is yourself, but they are wrong, and that path doesn't lead to joy and fulfillment.

God is the audience of one. If the only person you were trying to please this Christmas was God, how would this Christmas be different to every other Christmas? Place God at the center of your decisions, at the center of your days, at the center of Christmas, and have your Best Christmas Ever.

And remember... Find your joy. Cherish your joy. Guard your joy. And follow your joy.

25.
Choosing to Be Right Rather Than Happy.

It's not easy to have a great Christmas in a world where everyone is striving for what isn't worth having.

Obstacle #25 is: Choosing to be right rather than happy.

One of my oldest and best friends talks about this concept often. "Would you rather be right or happy?" he asks. Being right often doesn't change anything. Proving that you are right about something often requires an argument.

This Christmas make an active effort not to argue about things that don't really matter. Let it go. Let it be. Move on. Ask yourself, "Would you rather be right or happy?"

This Christmas... Find your joy. Cherish your joy. Guard your joy. And follow your joy.

26. Negativity.

It's not easy to have a great Christmas in a world where everyone is striving for what isn't worth having.

We are exploring twenty-eight obstacles that will prevent you from having your Best Christmas Ever.

Obstacle #26 is: Negativity.

Negativity is a major obstacle to having your Best Christmas Ever. This negativity enters into our lives in a number of ways. One enormous source of negativity in our lives is the news media. Take a break from reading, watching, and listening to the news for 48 hours and see how that impacts you. Do you feel more relaxed? More peaceful? More focused?

Another source of negativity is the content we consume. TV shows, books, movies, etc. Does the content you are consuming put you in a positive or negative space?

Then there is the content of daily conversation. Take

note. Are your conversations positive or negative?

And of course, we have our own negativity. Are you aware of when you are in a positive or negative space?

There are two other ways that we foster negativity that are worth mentioning here. Expecting the worst and not letting people change. Christmas is a season of hope. Foster hope in your expectations this year. And let people change. People want to change, but very often it is those who are closest to them who hold them back or create obstacles to the change they desire. Let people change. How? Experience them as if you were meeting them for the first time this Christmas. Ask them questions as if for the first time. Their answers may surprise you. Their answers will reveal how they have changed or how they desire to change.

Christmas is a time of possibilities. And Christians are the ultimate people of hope and possibilities.

And remember... Find your joy. Cherish your joy. Guard your joy. And follow your joy.

27.
Ego.

It's not easy to have a great Christmas in a world where everyone is striving for what isn't worth having.

Obstacle #27 is: Ego.

The capacity of our ego to ruin even the best things in life is limited. That's why we need to keep an eye on it. Like most things, you can't just throw it away. Because your ego does have a positive role and value in your journey. For example, the self-assurance provided by the ego is critical for us to press through difficult situations and accomplish what we feel called to. It provides a sense of self that is not dependent on external validation so that we can follow the star God has placed before us in life.

But the ego can get out of control and cause lots of problems. This is particularly true when it gets into the comparisons game, comparing you to others or others to you. This can lead to you falsely thinking

you are better than others or falsely believing that you are worse than others. In both situations the infinite intrinsic dignity and value of every human person gets lost.

The ego can also lead us to value the wrong things, leading us into all manner of vanities. It can lead us to get caught up in selfishness and self-loathing, and generally distract us from focusing on what matters most. It is impossible to have your best anything if you lose sight of what matters most.

And remember... Find your joy. Guard your joy. Follow your joy. Not just happiness. It seems our culture has confused happiness with comfort, and following comfort will lead you to misery. Find your joy. Cherish your joy. Guard your joy. And follow your joy.

28. Fear of Being Different.

It's not easy to have a great Christmas in a world where everyone is striving for what isn't worth having.

How has exploring these twenty-eight obstacles prepared you for Christmas? Are you ready to have your Best Christmas Ever?

Obstacle #28 is: Fear of being different.

The gentle voice within calls you toward the truest version of yourself and that will always be away from the crowd. If you are afraid of being different, that is okay. It's natural. It's normal. But it is time to overcome that fear and step into your truest self.

In what ways are you being called to be different this Christmas? In what ways are you being invited to be counter-cultural?

This Christmas... Find your joy. Cherish your joy. Guard your joy. And follow your joy.